Get Published Get Noticed

Author Means Authority! ™

Your Book is Your Expanded Business Card!

Shawn Chhabra
Five Times Bestselling Author

+

FREE CONSULTING OFFER

Keyword Search, Topic, Title, Writing, Formatting, Publishing -Digital Copies, Publishing-Print Version, Audio Version, Promotion and PR, AS-SEEN-ON- AFFILIATE NETWORKS (FOX, ABC, NBC, CBS, ETC.), Ongoing support
http://www.Get-Published-Get-Noticed.com/gpgn/

Table of Contents

FREE RESOURCES: We will provide you **Done-For-You, as well as Do-it-Yourself** packages.

We will help you with – Keyword Search, Topic, Title, Writing, Formatting, Publishing -Digital Copies, Publishing-Print Version, Audio Version, Promotion and PR, AS-SEEN-ON- AFFILIATE NETWORKS (FOX, ABC, NBC, CBS, ETC.), Ongoing support

http://www.Get-Published-Get-Noticed.com/gpgn/

Foreword

I am somebody just like you who was wondering what might be next in my career. I knew that publishing a book had great value, but I never really understood just how far that went. I was at a point in my life where I knew I had to take risks to get to the next level, and nothing seemed riskier than publishing my own book. I am living proof that you CAN do it, and that if you put your mind to it that you can make it work to your advantage.

Here's an important thing to know about me—I learned English as a second language. I came here with dreams but not much else, and then I transformed all of this into great success. What helped to make me a recognized name and really launch my career was to become a published author. Yes I did it, and that means that you can too! I am also here to tell you that you don't have to be a writer to turn your ideas into published work. If I can do it, so can you—and it is out of this experience that I have great insight to share.

So though you may think that I'm just an expert naturally or that I have a background in writing, know that this isn't true. I tell you this because I want you to understand just how accessible this can be. I have enjoyed amazing success by getting my work published, and therefore I want to help you to do the same. Don't let fear or inhibition get in the way of long term success, and know that in the end this can help you to get to where you want to be.

It worked for me and it can work for you—it's really that simple! I wrote this book to help others just like me and I hope that I reach to you when I walk you through the process. My experience is bound to help others and that's reward enough. So please read on and know that great things await you if you take the plunge into getting published, and it all starts now—so follow along with me!

A Little About Me…..

Who I am and why you should listen to me? Fair enough question, so let me introduce myself.

I'm an immigrant from India. English is not my first language. So I may have started off with what some may call a disadvantage, but I have really turned that into a successful entrepreneurial business. The idea here is that I've done it and you can too—and I want to share my knowledge, experiences, and insight with you!

Here's my list of credentials, and I tell you this because I think it plays well into my ability to teach you--

Serial Entrepreneur : I have seen enough – Restaurant business, Door to Door sales, Import/Export business, Christmas store, Social media and Online Marketing, as well as Leads Generation business, Computer and Consumer Electronics –Wholesale, Retails, and Online ecommerce business, Holistic Health Online College, Herbal Supplement business, Coaching and Mentoring, Authoring Books, Bestselling author of multiple books, and Publisher.

Five Time Bestselling Author: Writing/authoring and publishing have helped me to connect and network with celebrity status authors and business owners. Publishing has also helped me get PR exposure and teaching/mentoring opportunities. On top of this, one of the universities in California awarded me an honorary PhD Degree. My published book also provided me the opportunity to meet Mr. Mark Victor Hansen, the legendary co-creator of "Chicken Soup" book series.

Book Publishing has also provided me the platform to pursue my life time goal of helping others do what they like to do, and pursue their goals and achieve financial freedom. So not only have I benefited from my hard work and success, but I have the opportunity to help others along the way.

I always wanted to help others achieve success and reach their goals, while doing what they love to do and achieve financial freedom. I am in a position to do this. Now I am opening an online publishing and coaching school to help others get published.

Everything I've Done Has Taken Me To This Very Moment

A friend of mine, James Thomas, found out I have been enjoying great success in publishing and profiting from it. He approached me and wanted me to help him by showing him my successful publishing system. He wanted to understand my blueprint so that he could get all the benefits and profits of publishing a book. I was able to guide him in the right direction and he successfully published a collaborative book with seven other writers.

Here is a testimonial from James:

"Shawn has provided his wisdom, support, and assistance for every step of my book, HAPPINESS CHRONICLES: SHORT STORIES AND RECIPES FOR A HAPPY LIFE. I could have never accomplished this without his dedication and determination. Shawn also helped me get started with my own passive income business. Shawn is a true teacher and educator. If you need help with your business, there is no one better to call on." – Jim Thomas

I have learned wonderful life lessons and enjoyed great successes, and now I want to share that with my readers and followers. Everything that I have worked so hard for is playing out right in front of me. I want to share the secrets and tips of publishing, so that others may enjoy the same great success. So it is my hope that this book will help people to realize the true importance of publishing, and to understand what it takes to get there.

SPECIAL OFFER: FREE RESOURCES: We will provide you **Done-For-You, as well as Do-it-Yourself** packages.
We will help you with – Keyword Search, Topic, Title, Writing, Formatting, Publishing -Digital Copies, Publishing-Print Version, Audio Version, Promotion and PR, AS-SEEN-ON- AFFILIATE NETWORKS (FOX, ABC, NBC, CBS, ETC.), Ongoing support

http://www.Get-Published-Get-Noticed.com/gpgn/

Introduction

Are you at a point in your career where you want to take things to the next level? Do you have big aspirations of moving forward, but feel a bit unsure about how to get there? Though you might think that enjoying long term success is all about the traditional marketing activities, you more than likely are overlooking something key to your long term success—publishing your own book!

Yes I know that when you read that it may immediately send you into a tailspin. I know firsthand what it means to fear publishing or to feel that you are just not a good candidate for it. I am here to tell you though that you are capable of much more than you realize. If you put your mind to it and really start to embrace just how much publishing a book can do for you and your career, then you will enjoy some amazing success for it.

All You Need Is An Idea To Start With

The most surprising part of all of this is that you don't need to be an author. You can get help putting the right words on paper, that's not the hard part. If you have an idea, or if you happen to be a subject matter expert on something then that's the key to success. Jotting down some ideas is all it takes—and I will show you the process to then turn those ideas into a published piece of work that means instant success. People will know you, they will turn to you, and in the end you will enjoy some amazing success because of it.

I have been where you are right now, and I have had the same hesitation about publishing a book that you have. I can relate to everything that you're feeling, but I am also living proof that you can make it work for you. Don't let your own fear be what stands in the way of great success! Having a published book affords you things in life that you probably never dreamed possible. So take the leap and let's work through this together—then you can move forward with making this your reality and enjoying all that comes along with it.

Let's get started—and see how publishing can work for you and take you to a level you never dreamed possible!

You Will Learn What It Means To Successfully Publish

I'm going to share with you some tips and insight from my perspective. You need to first understand what the face of publishing looks like today. You want to be sure that you have answers to the most fundamental questions, and then you can take on this challenging but rewarding process. Getting yourself published is much more commonplace today than it was years ago, and that's because there are excellent resources available that we never had before.

Publishing can be a very rewarding process, because at the end of it all you have your finished product before you. I will walk you through the secrets to getting your book published, and then how to successfully share it with the world. I know that you may feel a bit of apprehension due to the uncertainty of it all—but I promise that once you invest your efforts into this whole process, it really will pay off tremendously!

Having the desire to get published is the first step, and if you're reading this book then you're already a step ahead of the game. Getting all the ideas written will help you to formulate a plan, get passionate about your subject matter, and the best is yet to come. You've already done the hardest part by writing the book—now it's time to understand what it takes to see it through and get it published so that you can help others and share your thoughts with the world!

Whether you are in business for yourself, a department head or just working for someone else, you can publish a book! Just think about it, if you do work for someone else and decide to write a book you can add that accomplishment to your resume which can help you move up in the company or go out and find a better job or career that you truly want.

Others will look at you as being an authoritative professional who knows exactly what he is talking about. Of course you definitely have to know what you are talking about and be genuine in your book. You can't just throw a book together and think you are going to become the best in the business. Bringing fresh ideas to the table and talking about the aspects that you know best will help you succeed. Figure out what you know best to explain it to your audience in complete detail. ***Your published book will be your showcase.***

You are here and that means -- Opportunity is knocking at your door!

Today is the day to get published!

Here's Your First Tip--
You can get published in two ways:
1. You can write and get published
2. You don't have to write, but you can still get published

Hard to believe, right?

It's Simple!
Make a Choice!
Start Now!
The Transformation Start Here!

The process of getting published will transform you as it's an amazing journey.

<u>Annika Sorensen, Published Author</u>

"I have always considered myself to be an excellent business woman, and I had accomplished some great things in my career. I had done well for a number of years, but had come to a point where I knew I needed to grow things just one step further—I just wasn't sure what that entailed. I had talked to marketing professionals and had a handle on what might work well, but in all honesty had never considered the notion of publishing my own book.

I came across Shawn's book and I will admit that the idea of publishing my own book was a little intimidating to me, really out of reach if I'm being honest. I knew I had great ideas and I knew that I had a lot of experiences and information to share—but I was definitely not a writer by trade. How could I be a published author? Well I found out all the secrets and best advice through Shawn's book, and I can't say enough about what I can do for you.

It doesn't matter what type of business you are in, what your skillset may be, or what walk of life you come from— you can get your ideas published too and it will launch your career in a whole new direction! I was amazed at how much new business I picked up because of getting published, and how people really turned to me. **This can happen for you too**, and using **Shawn's book** to help you to get there is key.

I can't say enough about how helpful Shawn's insight is, and I just love his approach. He's easy to follow and understand, and you relate to him because he has gone through much of the same ups and downs in his own career. I felt inspired by his story, and his insight really talked directly to me.

So if you are at a point where you really want to launch your career in a whole new direction, publishing is where it's at. If you haven't a clue about publishing your own book, or if you simply want some inspiration and ideas to get you going then Shawn's book is undoubtedly the best way to get to where you want to be. ***Kudos on a great book, and thanks for giving me the push I needed to move forward with this!"***

Shawn is a genuine guy who shoots people straight and is never willing to bend his integrity for the sake of his personal gain. You will find that Shawn is engaging and coaches out-side the box (a good thing) and pushes individuals to grow from within. **Shawn Chhabra is the go to expert** if you want to increase your visibility and rise above the noise. One of the sharpest and most competent individuals I've had the privilege to know.

*Publishing my book "**Take stress from chaos to calm**" is the biggest step up I have done in my business. All of a sudden everybody wants to talk to me about it. There is awe in their voices. The subject of the book was an easy decision. I just made a workbook out of my signature program – about things I know really well anyway. It ended up to be a workbook good to use for anybody AND at the same time I got an exclusive "business card" to give to my most important clients/prospects. I also use the book as work material in my workshops. Before I was just somebody working with stress management – now I am Dr Annika with a good workbook on stress management. If I can write a book – you can too! / Dr Annika at www.askdrannika.com*

Adam Barrett, Entertainment Guru

I attended a lunch **presentation with Shawn** about self-publishing, and was amazed at the scope of what he presented in such a short time, his expertise and the resources he presented. Shawn is a publishing and media guru. Would recommend his skills for anything you might need related book concept development, publishing as well as book marketing.
https://www.linkedin.com/profile/view?id=41465178

Adam Barrett, Entertainment Guru

Kay K. Larson

"I cannot think of a better person to help me market my book than Shawn Chhabra. Shawn is not only a great business person and thoroughly knows the publishing business, he is also kind, and compassionate and totally dedicated to helping his clients. It is so rare that you find that combination. He really wants me to succeed! I am secure in the knowledge that I am in the best hands with Shawn when it comes to fulfilling my life-long dream of becoming a successful author."
- Kay K. Larson, Author/Coach

ANKIT SAPRA

Shawn is a great business and personal development trainer and mentor. I attended Shawn's presentation: "How to Get Published and Use Your Book as an Expended Business Card," sponsored by Authority College. Shawn was able to present tons of information about book-publishing, from concept development to self-publishing and marketing your book.
If you are looking for more leads and clients for your business then getting published may be the short-cut you can use. Make a book your future, and consider Shawn as your guide. Shawn's warm personality makes the process even more enjoyable! Shawn is also a great business and personal development trainer and mentor.
ANKIT SAPRA, MBA

Patience Reich

Shawn Chhabra is the go to expert if you want to increase your visibility and rise above the noise.

- Patience was Shawn Sudershan's client
https://www.linkedin.com/profile/view?id=16609510
Patience Reich, MD, SFHM

Kathie Belfield

Shawn is an amazing author and has an incredible personality!

February 24, 2014, Kathie worked with Shawn Sudershan at shawnchhabra.com
Kathie Belfield (LinkedIn)

Owner at Memories Are Forever

Jim Thomas, Entrepreneur, Published Author

Shawn has provided his wisdom, support, and assistance for every step of my book, **HAPPINESS CHRONICLES: SHORT STORIES AND RECIPES FOR A HAPPY LIFE**. I could have never accomplished this without his dedication and determination. Shawn also helped me get started with my own passive income business. **Shawn is a true teacher and educator.** If you need help with your business, there is no one better to call on. – *Jim Thomas*

Ben Glaser, Business Student, Entrepreneur

I had just graduated college when I first met Shawn Chhabra. I was new to the business world and unsure of what I wanted to do. Through his guidance, experience and working side by side with him helped me figure out what my strengths were and what I need to pursue. I found what I am passionate about and every day I go to work is a great day that I enjoy. **It was truly life changing and lucky of me to meet Shawn and has undoubtedly changed my future and my success.**
Ben Glaser, UMSL Business Student, Entrepreneur

Free Consultation Offer: It is not possible to foresee every issue that may arise when you write and publish your book. You are welcome to reach out and ask our team for assistance. Please visit our websites for help.

http://www.Get-Published-Get-Noticed.com/gpgn/
http://shawnchhabra.com/

Copyright Notice

Publisher: www.ShawnChabra.com

Author: Shawn Chhabra

Illustrated by: Tameisha Harrington

You may already be feeling doubtful and you may even be thinking:

"Who Me?" "A Published Author?" "Bestseller?" "Seen In Major Media"—It simply can't be possible, can it? **You may be thinking that this is some sort of a joke or a prank?** You may even think that I'm crazy, but this is real life—and this can become your success story and reality if you go about it the right way!

It's All About Having Expertise or a Vision—Then The Rest Is Easier Than You Think

You may also feel like you're in the thick of "writer's block", or you may even be thinking that you don't like to write anyhow. Maybe you're not even an avid reader, or even like books. I will tell you that I myself hated books during my school days, and now I love them after my own personal experience! Just because you don't love books or feel that you're not the strongest writer doesn't necessarily mean that you can't be a successful and accomplished writer.

I turned my thoughts into words, and before I knew it I had a full fledged story before me that evolved into a bestselling book. It can start with being a subject matter expert in something or having some thoughts or ideas to share. It just starts with a vision or an expertise that you think would benefit others. Just having the dream or vision is the first step, and then you have to learn what to do to make it work—and that's precisely what you'll do here!

If I understand your mindset accurately, then this book is for you. If you find that you are somebody who finds the idea of a published book to be exciting, but never thought it would come from you then you're not alone. **This book is exactly written keeping you and people like you in mind.**

You don't like to write? – Not a Problem
You will not write? – Not a Problem
We have created a system to get you published and you'll profit from it. Our system and our team are here to help you get successfully published and promoted. **We are here to help you throughout the entire publishing journey!**

I'm Here To Help Those Who Need A Path Defined For Them

Think of it this way – the authors or full time writers already have a sense of how to write and how to get published. They either have experience in this area, or they know the right person to reach out to in order to make it happen. *They're not the segment of the market for which this book was written for.*

Those who already write for a living or who spend a great deal of their time writing or publishing already have the secrets—so I write this book for those of you like me who have a great idea or a desire to get published, but up until now felt fearful, unsure, or never really considered that publishing might actually be in your future somehow.

So do you want to know who my real audience is? Are you interested in why I have put together a sort of "how to" book to navigate your way through getting your ideas published? I do have a valid reason and it is to help the segment of the market that wish to get published, but either don't know it yet or don't know how to really get started.

I am writing this book for "non-writers" who are interested in one or more of the following in their life and their professional achievements. I write this book for those who want to or need help with:

- ***Achieving Instant Expert, Celebrity, and Hero Status***: You may want to be famous or at least get your name out there. By getting a book published you will be the type of person that people look up to, that people respect, and you will become a celebrity even within a small niche. To those who have always wanted to be looked to as a subject matter expert or generally as a big deal, I want to help you get there through a credible path towards getting published and building a name and reputation for yourself. I will get you there!

- ***Build More Credibility:*** You know that you have important things to say and you recognize that getting published will help to really build your reputation. You want to have this accomplishment behind your name, for it speaks to your credibility in a whole new way. You want to be the one who stands out from the crowd for having a published book which makes you an expert and a very credible source on the subject matter at hand.

- ***Develop Your Business Further:*** You are taking your business as far as you can go, and you know that having a published book is the next natural step. You may know what you want to say or what message you want to share with the mainstream audience, but feel that you aren't capable of writing it yourself. You see the value in getting published as it will truly help you to take your business to the next level in so many new and unique ways.

- ***Develop More Or Add New Leads:*** Not only can you help to expand your business by having a published book, but you can also **attract new clients**. I don't care what type of business you are in, if you can point to a book that you got published it's going to attract attention. You will add to the new leads and really build upon referrals because people look to you as a true subject matter expert—and that means that they want to work with you and help to support you.

- ***Charging Higher Rates From New And Even Existing Clients:*** Though you're certainly not going to swindle your existing clients, you do need to use this additional accomplishment as a means by which you can generate revenue. You are essentially worth more when you get your expertise out there to share with the world. Most of your established clients will recognize this and will be willing to pay the extra money because you are now a published author. For new clients it's a "no brainer" for they see that they are going to work with somebody who really knows their stuff—and they want to be part of it!

- **More Coaching and Speaking Opportunities:** Never underestimate the potential *opportunities that await* you once you get published. You probably don't even realize it yet, but when people read your book they are going to want to hear you speak. They are going to look to you as a coach or a mentor, and therefore they are going to want to pay to get the extra help or support. This can mean increased revenue for you, and a possible career path that you may have never considered before.

- **Earn More Respect:** Maybe you want more respect, or maybe you're not even looking for it but will find it. The point is that once you are a published author it puts you into a certain category. Once you get your word out there people respect you and want to emulate you, and therefore you are a smart and savvy business professional in every sense of the word. Respect is earned, and getting your work published gets you that and allows you certain privileges because of it.

The Possibilities Are Endless

There are Billions of people (prospects) connected to Internet enabled devices (PC's, Laptops, Tables, Smart Phones and Kindle, Nook and many more devices). Companies with a large established infrastructure, like, Apple, Google and Amazon will help you to share your message (through your book) to those prospects.

Your prospects will have instant access to you and be able to reach you, your team and your network of existing clients—and ultimately that will help you close more deals. Existing clients will pay you more as you are their hero and proven subject expert. This will also help you get more local clients due to your celebrity status and credibility. People will know who you are, what you know, and they will want to be associated with or work with you. Every single book, in the hands of your prospects and clients will work like your sales team, and that book will be your calling card to selling more products and services. You are about to create your very own sales team. Any time someone will see your book on the book shelf or their desk, they will think of you and eventually buy from you.

There is so much great potential just from having your ideas published that you will see that there is nothing else that can add as much value to your business and your name!

You can write a book to support your existing business or you can just write a book, and then create a business around that book. What you may not realize is that your business will grow faster than you could ever imagine due to the added credibility you will receive as a published author and therefore perceived expert.

Once you are a published author, you are an expert, an authority, and a celebrity in your own right. All of your credibility is associated with your business and the expertise that you bring to the bottom line or subject matter.

Your existing clients will be willing to pay you more as you will be seen as being worth more than you were before. You probably don't believe that one because it sounds too good to be true, but there is great value in your written word being shared with the world.

There's More Value Than You Ever Imagined Possible

Prospects will buy from you (and your business) as you will **stand out from the crowd** (crowd of your competitors). Your closing ratio will increase dramatically. You are the **"go to person"** in this niche, and you will start to see that reflected in your sales and new leads.

You will not need to convince anyone to buy from you, because they will ultimately be chasing you to connect with you and buy from you. **Yes you will control your own destiny** and you will grow leaps and bounds beyond other marketing methods, all due to getting your published word out there to share with the world!

Look around you and you will notice that so called top experts and rich people have been using their books to grow their credibility and business. They didn't all do the writing themselves, but rather they had the idea and went for it!

YOU MAY BE THINKING THAT YOU HAVE NO INTENTION OF BEING AN ENTREPRENUER.
Here's why you may want to rethink your strategy and really focus on what this can do for your business in a whole new fresh way.
Get published and then update your resume' and use your books or references to your books in each section such as:
Education >>> Your Published Book Listed Here Along With Your Expertise
Experience >>> You Have Established Experience and Expertise Here and Your Book Will Showcase That
Certifications >>> Yes You Have Some Serious Credentials Here As You Are a Published or Even Best Selling Author
Trade References >>> This Is a Perfect Spot To Reference Your Published Book

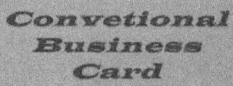

BOOK
(CARD)
GET SAVED
AS VALUABLE
DOCUMENT

This Is Your Time To Shine

There is never a wrong time or occasion to talk about your published book. Now you see how much value and how many potential opportunities await you if you follow the path towards being a published author. Now you see that in order to be a credible and highly successful entrepreneur, that you almost need a published book to add to your credibility. There is truly no better way to show off your know how and to share with the world what you know and how much value you can add!

It really does work, and now you need to understand the ins and outs so that you can be successful and profit from all this expertise! I am going to help you through the process, to understand how it all works, and ultimately ensure that you make this a successful venture in your own life.

We will help you in overcoming writer's block and in setting goals that work for you. We will also help you with time management and procrastination problems. **You only have to possess the desire and drive to make this work, and then I will help you to get there!**

So let's move forward with understanding the process, and then approaching this step by step so that you are set up for publishing and long term success!

Being A Published Author Means...

I AM SMART!

I AM AN EXPERT!

I AM RESPECTED!

I AM CREDIBLE!

What Is Book Publishing?

You become an author by writing a book. Book publishing is when the book is written and published. Therefore, you have to create, produce, distribute and promote your book. So it's a process and you have to think through one step at a time, but it will ultimately be very rewarding when it works out.

There are different types of book publishing from traditional book publishing, to self-publishing, to independent publishing, to vanity, and subsidy publishing. **Understanding the differences between the various types is the first step**. Then being honest with yourself with what you are capable of, or better yet what will make a good fit for your needs and long term goals is another. This will help you to break it all down and to pursue the path towards publishing that makes the most sense.

Self Publishing
You may try self-publishing which takes a lot of work. You will basically have to do almost everything yourself from marketing to distributing, which can be very costly and time-consuming. If you know what you're doing or have been through the process before it works well, but not usually the best path for the novice. You may find that after successfully publishing once that you want to venture into this type, and it may work well for you then.

Traditional Book Publishing

Traditional book publishing is when a book publishing company purchases an author's manuscript. They will handle everything for you and there is very little money put upfront, if at all. **You can approach the publishing company yourself by sending your manuscript or get an agent to submit the manuscript for you**.

Many individuals try to get their books published every day, most are unsuccessful. So yes you may not necessarily have great odds by approaching the publisher directly, but it can work. **If you find that you are having no luck, then it may be time to enlist the help of a professional in this area as well.**

Some Professional Outside Help

Most book publishers prefer working with an agent rather than the author. **Some agents will want an upfront fee to work for you, or simply get a portion of the book royalties after it is published.** The right agents are very helpful in getting you the best deal, because they guide you every step of the way. They know the ins and outs of the business, the right editors to speak to, as well as the trends in the industry – what's hot, what's not.

The best agent knows the steps to take after being accepted to be published from negotiating the book production process to the sales agreement and more. You want to find the right agent who will give you the best advice and outcome for your book deal. Of course, you can try to go at it alone, but you may not get the best deal for yourself, get rejected or may not even get a response at all.

Do your homework, not only into the type of publishing that best suits you but also the agent that is the best fit. If you are careful about this and choose wisely then this will help you to get your book to market – and that makes for a successful strategy overall!

Your book does not have to be long, just long enough to deliver your message. You want to go from general to specific areas of your expertise to showcase what you have ascertained.

'Publishing, or perhaps I ought to say, Book-Publishing, is quite different from what most people apparently suppose. The young man who regards it as a pleasantly dilettante occupation suitable for somebody who does not know what he wants to do but likes books, is under an illusion.' Stanley Unwin, THE TRUTH ABOUT PUBLISHING (1960 edition).

You might wonder why so many more people are moving towards publishing. You may even wonder why the publishing world has blown up so much in recent years. It seems that nearly everyone has a published book—and so it makes you wonder what has changed on this landscape so drastically. **The bottom line is that publishing today is very different, and so more and more people are recognizing the true power in it and jumping on board.**

What has more people involved in publishing? Why is it so much easier to get published? Why has the publishing industry become even more lucrative? There are a variety of reasons for the changes on the publishing landscape, and it's time to learn how these changes in today's world can benefit you and how you need to key in on them. **Here is what sets publishing apart in today's world--**

- **You don't have to be a writer to get published:** This is a huge distinction and what makes publishing so much more accessible than it used to be. Sure you may find that you are at a great advantage if you are a writer, but you don't necessarily have to be. You can hire a ghostwriter or even pitch your idea and get somebody else to bring it to life. There are so many tools and methods out there to get your ideas published, without ever actually writing a word on your own.

- *You have many options available to you in terms of publishing and how to bring it to market:* As we talked about you can go the route of self-publishing or even of traditional publishing with some help. With the online evolution of publishing you can even customize a package that works best for you.

  It's accessible, there are many options out there, and therefore more and more people can take advantage. So no matter who you are, what your thoughts that you want to share may be, or what you hope to accomplish out of publishing, you can get that visibility in a number of different ways now.

- *Publishing is so much more common and yet so much more impactful:* You are going to get some serious value out of your published book. We've talked about the benefits, and so there's really great reason as to why it's so much more common. Yes every celebrity and business authority has a book—and that means that you can too! Knowing that you don't have to do the writing or the editing really helps to shed some light onto how you can make this work.

- ***A published book means so much more power and revenue today than it ever used to:*** It used to be that publishing was something out there only for a certain group of people. Only the elite or the true writers got published, and so many of us never even thought about it. Nowadays you get so much more traction and value out of publishing and therefore you will find it to be a great fit in your overall business model.

  You can't go wrong by getting published, as it will bring a great deal to your bottom line. That is perhaps the biggest change and transformation, that the accessibility and true impact having published work brings makes it an intricate part of the overall marketing strategy!

<u>Free Consultation Offer</u>: It is not possible to foresee every issue that may arise when you write and publish your book. You are welcome to reach out and ask our team for assistance. Please visit our websites for help.

http://www.Get-Published-Get-Noticed.com/gpgn/
http://shawnchhabra.com/

So why should YOU publish a book? What is it that the world will want to learn from you specifically? This may be the biggest question to overcome and answer, and therefore present itself as the most obvious initial obstacle.

Once you can get to the heart of this and really answer honestly why you want to publish, and what information you have to share then it's smooth sailing from there. *The "why" is the most pivotal question to answer*, and it will help you to focus accordingly and to get excited.

The most obvious reason to publish is to share your knowledge or opinion on a given subject. A book can be written to enlighten, inspire, give direction or instruction, give an opinion, share facts and viewpoints.

You Have Something To Share With The World

So if you happen to be somebody who is well versed or experienced in a given area, then you can share that information and insight with the world. If you are somebody who has a very unique point of view on something that can help others, then that's another great reason to share with the world through your written word.

The reasons for publishing will vary, and it's a very individual thing. There's no right or wrong here—the only wrong would be in keeping from publishing because you are afraid. There is nothing to lose and everything to gain if you have information, facts, or a point of view that may benefit somebody. Whether it's an educational book, a "how to" book, or just something to document your experience or point of view—you can benefit from publishing and so can your readers!

Books can make someone laugh or cry, make you angry or sad. There is so much to learn from, as well as to potentially gain valuable insight from a well written book. Most people learn something from reading books.

So keep that in mind as books aren't solely for entertainment, but also to help shed light on something that can benefit others. You never know what you may find beneath the cover—and that gives you some great opportunity as a potential publisher of your own book!

Are You Frequently The One Who Is Asked Questions?

Do co-workers or employees often come to you with questions about starting a project or trying to get it complete? How many times have you had to stop what you were doing to help on a new project? Do you make suggestions that will help speed up the process or get it done in a more efficient manner? Do you number crunch to save money to come in under budget on a particular task?

Think about these things because even when you are simply the "**go to person**" in your workplace, that can help to create the basis for why you should get published. Have you failed at a project, but kept going to knock out the bugs that were holding up progress? Sometimes it takes learning from failure to help you to be your best! Sometimes it's simply a matter of putting all of your ideas, point of view, and insight into written words that helps you and others to see just how much you really do know. If people are coming to you to ask you questions, then that's something special.

Being on top of things to keep them flowing smoothly and productively means that you truly know what you are doing and how to get things done. You have a sense of accomplishment once the project is completed satisfactorily. You may not even realize just how insightful you are until you take a step back. When you stop and think about it, you may really have more knowledge and know how than you ever imagined.

You may very well be the one in control and not even recognize that until you try to search for a reason to get published. Not only can this help to take your business skills to the next level, but it may also serve as a new opportunity that you had never even considered as well. This is your time to shine, your opportunity to share all of that knowledge with the world, and there is no better time than now to get your word out there—great things lie ahead for you if you happen to be the one answering all the questions!

Take Your Knowledge and Skills To The Next Level

When you are deciding to write your book what do you want your readers to draw from it? Is it something that will help them with their job, career, lifestyle, health, family, or relationship? There should be some question to answer or some specific insight to share—you want to stand out from the crowd and therefore you want to keep that in mind as you think through your reasons and purpose for publishing.

You must know what you are talking about in order to write a book to help and inspire others. If you have practiced your craft and feel others can benefit from what you have learned, then writing a book would be the best way to do that.

You already know something and have great experience in some area – everyone has or knows something special. So why hide that from the world? Why not consider taking that knowledge to the next level? If you have a special skill or know how to solve a certain problem, then it serves you well to share that with others in a really profound way.

Something That You Know Can Enlighten Others In Some Way

Everyone has some experience, some personal viewpoint, or some insight to share from their life, their career, or their relationships. So identify it and then let this power you forward and keep you motivated as you think of what shape your book will take on.

Everyone from family to friends to neighbors to people thousands of miles away will look upon you as a hero. You will be sought after for your tenacity and true comprehension in the industry. Your book should inspire or enlighten others to achieve their goals and keep them motivated to want to do more.

Writing a book is an exercise, and you will discover a new self in the process of writing. You will know more about yourself as crazy as that may seem. Your book will provide your perspective about the industry you are in. Focus on your core work experiences and expertise, as well as the areas you wish to be seen as an expert.

It can educate and enrich many that may not have thought about a certain idea or outcome. There is something that you can share with the world which will help to enlighten them, or at the very least challenge them to think. *You can make a difference and it all starts here!*

Show Others What You Know!

Let everyone in the office know what you can truly do and bring to the table. You have to conduct yourself as a leader. Show that you are an authority in the industry, because putting it into the written word speaks volumes. Be factual and accurate in the things you do, say and the steps you take. If you are thoughtful in the words that you write and the point of view that you share or the way that you share it, then you will really help to bring your ideas forth in the right way. This is your opportunity to show others what you know, and therefore to make every word of it count—this is why you publish a book!

Without being overbearing or acting as a "know-it-all", you can display your skills and share your wisdom with the confidence that you exude. Take control by being authoritative which means being clear, concise and confident. Don't be afraid to share what you have to say, but just be sure that you're not being contrite or condescending. It's all about balance and it's important to give thought to the book and approach it with confidence—then people will love to read what you have to say.

When you submit new ideas and concepts to bring in clients, grow the business and keep everything on the up and up, others will respect you and follow suit. It will encourage them to be better workers and to do all they can to help out. There is no need to lecture or be extremely stern, just guide and support efforts to pull things together for the ultimate goal that you want to achieve. The goal will vary, and that's a good thing, but the point is that you go for it and publishing is the path to get you to where you want to be.

Lead by example, motivate by delegating, increase morale by getting others involved in what is going on. Strategically plan what needs to be done—and then get it done! You should know about everything that is going on, by following up and determining if the steps are working and the plan is coming together as scheduled in a proficient manner. Be the boss and assertively inject the proper insight to tackle what needs to be done. Feel good about what you are putting out there, and let your written words be a reflection of the person and professional that you are.

Add Value to Your Career!

Publishing a book can add great value to your career. **It will show that you know the industry and have the knowledge to succeed.** You will obviously want to know what other books are out there and write newer fresher content on the valuable skills and knowledge that you have obtained. It would be even better if the book has a whole new perspective than what is already out there.

You want to be the first to bring your ideas to market, or at the very least you want to stand out from the crowd. There's a very good chance that you will have competition and others will have published books on the very same subject, but if you can manage to stand out from the others then you will be successful so keep that in mind always.

By publishing a book or even two will showcase your leadership skills, your desire to succeed big and courage to take command and stand apart from others. You could gain new clients without even knowing them or having to speak to them directly. No sales pitch to try to win them over—that's how powerful your book can be for you!

They would be able to determine the kind of person you are and the type of business you run just from reading your book. After reading your book others will recommend you to their family, friends and co-workers. You will have created a wider and growing audience of potential new clients to do business with.

If you are struggling with your career or if you simply want to take things to the next level, publishing a book is how to get to where you want to be. ***Don't get too caught up in your own head or let outside influences sway you.***

This is YOUR opportunity to get your word out there, to add true value to what you do, and to get others to notice you in a really effective way—that's when you grow your business or even grow as an individual so be ready for it!

Major Benefits To Publishing

So just in case you need another reminder as to just how effective publishing can be for you, let this list be your guide. If you need that little extra push, if you find that you are struggling to get motivated, or if you feel unsure about what YOU can share with the world then surely one of these reasons can help. Here are the major benefits to getting published, and therefore what will help you to decide why you should publish in the first place.

- *You can use your book as a powerful business card (Foot in the Door Strategy): This* can be your calling card or a very active version of your business card. People will look at your book and see expertise and true conviction, and this not only means respect but translates to sales and revenue. No matter what the subject area may be, your book is the most powerful tool to use when first meeting somebody or to give them as a "leave behind" so that they are thinking of you.

- *Books sales can bring passive income (marketing the book actively):* You can use your book to help market your business and yourself. You can even get more income that comes to you without even having to work for it, because your book is just that powerful. So you can be making income just by having your book out there, as people will come to know you and therefore want to be a part of what you have to share.

- ***Constant supply of hot leads (using book with opt in strategies):*** You have a pipeline right there before you, and therefore you can grow your business in a whole new way. You may not even have to perform other marketing tasks for awhile, for your book can speak for you and your skills in a way that no other marketing tool possibly can. The leads will likely keep coming too!

- ***More coaching and speaking gigs:*** Even if you never thought about coaching or speaking engagements, you will get the opportunities like never before. People will want to come hear you speak on your given expertise, and this can manifest itself to a whole new career opportunity. Once you perform just one speaking engagement, people will respect you and your career will take off in a really great new way.

- *"PR"- lots of exposure to your business*: Want to build publicity for yourself and your business? Any expert in the field will tell you that it starts with a book these days. You get press, you get publicity, you get instant advertising, and all by using this one tool. You may not even need a standard press kit anymore, for a book is your calling card to building publicity and a reputation in the marketplace.

- *You are a local hero (lot more local leads)*: People love it when a local professional gets published as it brings the area pride. Not only that but you get more business on a local level, because people love to support local businesses in this day and age. So not only do you get greater visibility to the masses, you become a legitimate sensation within the local market and that's hard to come by!

- *Your Mom and Dad (and whole town) will be proud of you*: Yes there is a certain sense of pride when somebody that you know gets published. Don't forget that when you have the support and admiration from those closest to you, this does something to you as a person. When your closest family and friends are proud of you, it just builds your confidence and motivation that much more. This really does matter on a personal and even professional level!

- ***Your name will rule Google Searches:*** People love to find good content and authors through a well conducted Google search. Try to Google my name, Shawn Chhabra, and see the proof. It's not only rewarding to you to see your name as a top search result on Google, but others will really buy into this too. In the end--**PROSPECTS WILL FIND YOU AND HIRE YOU!**

'It is not enough to publish a good and marketable book, or even a number of them; I feel that one of the best advertisements for a publishing firm is for that firm to develop a distinct character which shall become recognized by the trade and the public.' Memo from T. S. Eliot to his fellow directors at Faber, 9 December 1931.

Is This The Next Natural Step For You?

You might be sitting there needing that little extra push. You may have the motivation and desire, but wonder if this truly is the next right step for you. This is a situation that so many of us face, and the reality is that if you have any inkling to do this for yourself or if your business could benefit from it at all—then yes, this is absolutely the next right step for you without a doubt!

If you're giving this thought and if you're wondering if this might be right, then it has some merit on some level. You have nothing to lose by doing this, and everything to gain. But is now the right time? Is it feasible that you could really do this? Are you ready to take this leap in hopes that it pays off? Yes you are, and if you can just ignore that inner voice of doubt then you can make it work. **The only thing standing in the way of your success is YOU—** so don't let that happen!

So is now the right time and is this the next step for you in your professional or personal life? Can you take possible rejection and let the potential benefits win out over that? Are you worried but yet exhilarated by the possibilities that this may afford you? There is so much to gain out of making this move, and so this very well could be the next natural step. **Here's how to be sure that this is right for you and that it will truly benefit you in the way that you want it to.**

- **Is there an area for which you feel you have a great deal of knowledge?** Are you that sort of "go to" person? Are you the person that can shed some light on things for others and therefore you feel like you really know your stuff?

  If you tend to be somebody who quickly grasps new concepts or who has a great deal of knowledge on things, then you are by far in the best place to publish your thoughts. This can really help you to get to the next level in a really profound new way, so why not go for it and see what wonderful things may lie ahead with sharing your knowledge with the world?

- **Are you the "go to person" or subject matter expert in a particular niche?** If people really value your opinion and respect your knowledge, then you are a built in subject matter expert. If you are the person that simply has the answers and therefore is so on top of things that others can't possibly go elsewhere, then this is your time to shine.

It usually stems out of having some great knowledge and then wanting to share that with others. This role may even happen quite naturally for you and all without you even trying. So if you want to show that you have the know how or if you truly have a great deal of knowledge in a given area, then you are truly a subject matter expert and you need to get this all out for others to see once and for all.

- **Are you looking to grow your business or your career to the next level?** You may be doing quite well but know that you need to grow things and take them to the next level. You may even be the type of person who recognizes that you have come to a crossroads and you need to move above and beyond.

  If you're not afraid of what this might bring you and you recognize that it's a good path towards getting what you want, then this can work quite well for you. This can be the one thing that helps you to grow your business in a really unique way!

- **Do you want to share your information and insight with the world to help others?** You may very well want to help others, and this can be a great way to do so. Your book may serve as a "how to" or at least help to give people great insight on a given topic. You may have great tips, information, or insight that can benefit the lives of others. Whatever you know a lot about, having the desire and therefore ability to share it with the rest of the world is truly what it's all about. This can really benefit you, but also benefit others and that may be what's driving you towards it in the end.

- ***Are you ready to challenge yourself in a way that could mean great long term benefits?*** You are going to push yourself outside of your comfort levels and never let anything stand in your way again.

  You are going to strive for great accomplishments in a way that isn't comfortable or familiar to you, but will bring you great success. This can be the secret to your success as you are challenging yourself in a compelling and really wonderful way—and you will experience personal growth that you never dreamed of!

A book that is published to entertain or take an individual on a fantasy makes for a great read, but publishing a book to gain credibility in this competitive world is a necessity these days. **Your published book will complement your business**, and that's an important point to focus on. You could potentially bring in huge profits, and generate leads in a really unique and successful way. If you never really knew what the next step was to grow and solidify your business, now you can see that publishing a book is all of that and so much more.

You want everyone to see what your business is about, but more importantly you want to write on a topic that you are passionate about, and for which you have detailed knowledge about and experience with. You are intimate with these topics, you are close to them, and you live and breathe them. You know what these topics are all about in a way that few others do—and that makes for an excellent springboard to move forward with!

Think about it, **it's your business and who knows more about your business than you?** You have all these thoughts bottled up inside you, so this is your outlet to let it out and share it with the world. There were lessons learned, big and small, obstacles that you overcame, a failure or two that could have wiped you out, but you kept at it. Within this knowledge is likely a story that others will be able to relate to or enjoy. Out of your life experiences others can gain something very real.

The words that you **write in your book should motivate and generate a buzz.** It should capture the attention of readers so they will want to read the whole thing as well as come to you to perhaps pick your brain even more. Putting your expertise in written form and having it published is significant. **People will want to do business with you simply because you have written what you know in book form and got it published.**

Not many people can say they have published a book, especially business owners. You have no idea how much power you have, and how others will benefit from it. You can't possibly understand the real magnitude of all of this until you put the wheels in motion. The end result is going to be truly amazing, so go for it and see what wonderful things come out of this! Wouldn't it be great to add author to your title?

Reinforce Your Credibility

You want your book to have a distinct advantage over all the other similar books already in the marketplace. Be creative and passionate and show all that you know. The drive, dedication and determination should come shining through. Now is the time to explain your ideas with authority. You don't know what you're capable of until you put it out there for the world to see. There is some truly amazing things ahead for you, so having the courage to go down this path will benefit you greatly.

You should trigger an emotion in the reader that will propel them into believing they have what it takes to succeed as well. This will strike a cord that will enhance your credibility. Just remember to always be genuine and straight forward. Write in a language that readers will understand and really grasp a hold of. Don't dumb it down, but also don't speak at a level that others can't find relatable. It's all about finding that balance that the readers will appreciate and grasp.

Be confident in your writing so you will come across as the "go to" authority and expert. Tangible evidence makes a story more believable and more convincing. You will also gain credibility from reviews. In addition, favorable and positive reviews will make you believable as a writer who knows what he is talking about. **You could also be featured on different media outlets, from television interviews to radio talk shows to Youtube.**

Experts are always in demand and they get the interviews because people want to hear what they have to say. Think of experts that you have seen featured in publications or media outlets—they all started from somewhere too and you can be the success story that others are talking about too!

Once your book is written and you get rave reviews or start appearing on media outlets, you could become a consultant or motivational speaker. When a potential client visits your website and sees that you have been interviewed or that there is so much positive feedback on your book, they will seek your expertise and want to do business with you. Others may simply want to pick your brain or assistance in writing a book. You could even go on to write another book or two!

This can foster some of the greatest success possible. Sure you got to where you're at through experience and hard work, but now moving forward means that you are focused on what it takes to go one step further. Don't let worry get in your way, just recognize how much great success can come out of this one activity to share with the world in a profound new way.

The main purpose is to communicate the results achieved were exponential toward continuous growth for you and the company. They will see that you are full of plans and perspectives. Your success will show others how you overcame obstacles and problems to become the successful person you are today. Not only will the potential client or customer see how you made it, but by telling them everything that you went through to reach the top level displays to them that you did not give up and that you are a go getter. You want them to believe, understand and benefit from your knowledge.

Writing may be art, but publishing, when all is said and done, comes down to dollars.
- Nicholas Sparks

Branding yourself is nothing more than having name recognition as an expert. You need more than talent to get ahead. Putting in hard work is good, but by becoming an expert author you have already branded yourself. The challenge was there and you took action to achieve the results that you wanted. **You became the expert and authority.**

Your brand is your reputation, your calling card, and the very essence of who you are. A good solid brand helps you to be successful. Think of some of the most well known brands that you know and use in everyday life—they all started with an idea or a concept or a product and then transformed into something much more than that. The same can hold true for your own personal brand, you can become that household name or authority that others look to in a really unique way.

To Establish Your Brand a Book Is an Excellent Tool to Use

A book is **the best marketing tool** to demonstrate to the masses what you can do for them; how you have achieved great success from simply branding your name and getting it out there. You will be able to show the hottest concepts in today's market as well as the biggest trends in your business industry. So if you want to unlock the true potential of your own personal brand, it all starts with a great book to boost your reputation and increase awareness.

Your brand is what establishes you in the market place. Chances are you've already made some strides towards establishing a brand if you have undertaken any marketing. Even if you have just worked hard at generating leads and tried to gain new business, you have worked at building or establishing a brand. So this is simply a matter of taking things to the next level, and that matters greatly in the big picture and your ability to market yourself and your business—and the book that you create will help you with this in a whole new way!

Publishing A Book Is Your Main Branding Strategy

Not only will readers want to become your clients, but the competition will look at your success and try to emulate it. You have already gone through the challenges, climbed up from the bottom and now your book will allow others to see all that can be done to be a great success story. You want people to look to your brand when they have a problem or service they need that you can assist with. Convey your **clear vision and mission** along with your hardcore values to enlighten others.

You are the brand, you are the authority, and you are the person that others want to look to. If this is already happening in everyday life for you, then you know how this feels. If it is something that you still need to explore or solidify, then nothing will build your brand quite like publishing your own book. Admittedly it's a huge step, but a really amazing one when it comes to fruition. You are in control of building your brand through this extensive step, and so it's time to progress with it.

By thrusting yourself into doing due diligence and making your mark in the business industry, you have exemplified a creative way to enhance your business and brand yourself accordingly. Focus on your marketable skills, as this will always serve you well. Personal branding will get you seen and noticed by others as an instant expert. You don't want others to rebrand you, so once you build your brand you must stay committed to strengthening and protecting it.

Build trust with your customers, engage them, give them what they want and need, be unique and honest to show you care. Your whole brand has to start consistent and stay consistent no matter what. Remember **your brand is your business!**

Being A Published Author Means...

I AM SMART!

I AM AN EXPERT!

I AM RESPECTED!

I AM CREDIBLE!

Being A Published Author Means...

I AM SMART!

I AM AN EXPERT!

I AM RESPECTED!

I AM CREDIBLE!

So **you finally see the credibility behind publishing** your own book. You see how this can help you to take your business, your brand, and your very self to the next level. Though you may have recognized this before, you now know without a doubt that this is the way to go. You will gain some really great visibility from all of this, and therefore it will serve as your best marketing tool possible. So how do you proceed from there?

As with anything it's best to take it **one step at a time**. If you look at publishing your own book as one huge task then it's going to be completely overwhelming. If instead you can think through what you need to do one activity at a time, then you will be far more successful. This will help your focus, ensure that you don't take on more than you should at a time, and also help you to get organized and stay on task.

Here are some helpful tips to ensure that you take this all one step at a time and therefore enjoy long term success out of publishing. It really can work, and this can work as a sort of **checklist** for you as you move along.

- *Consider what your main focus will be*: You have an idea or something to start the process in your mind, so consider what it is. Whatever your idea starter may be, no matter how big or small, this will form the path towards success. Consider what niche, what area, what expertise or skill you want to focus on for your main idea of the book. Just identifying this will help you to get started and move in the right direction, and that's all it takes!

- ***Get your ideas onto paper, just as an initial overview***: This doesn't mean that you have to actually write the book, but rather that you just get ideas down on paper. Put pen to paper and write what you want to focus on and any stream of consciousness. Consider this to be a sort of brainstorming session, for that is what will count in getting you heading in the right direction.

  Just develop your idea a bit and then you will have a path towards moving things forward. If you're not the writer, at least coming up with an outline or overview of topics will be key to your success with this.

- ***Align yourself with the right resources and tools to bring your ideas to life***: If you plan to hire a ghostwriter or just an editor, search for one. Put together your plan of attack and ensure that you align yourself with all the right resources to make it successful. You might need a good writer, a thorough editor, or simply a good agent or publishing house.

   Consider how in depth you will get with the actual writing or activities and what you will outsource. Once you know this then you can plan for your needs and ensure that you get it altogether in a comprehensive way—all part of the plan!

- ***Consider how the publishing process will work for you***: Everyone approaches publishing differently and that's a good thing. What works for one person may not work for you, so just consider making this process work in the best possible way for you. If you don't have a lot of writing experience then self - publishing may not work for you. Do your research and figure out which type of publishing will best fit your needs and skills, and then make a plan to integrate this important step.

- ***Get the word out and market your book as a successful business tool***: Though your book will eventually market itself, you need to put forth some effort initially. You will want to put thought into your marketing strategy so that you know how to get the word out that you have a published book. You want your current clients to know about it and you want to use it for further lead generation.

The sooner that you have a strategy in place to tell others that you are a published author, the sooner you will see your business succeed. Thinking through this in advance in a proactive manner will help you to enjoy some really great and lasting success!

Free Consultation Offer: It is not possible to foresee every issue that may arise when you write and publish your book. You are welcome to reach out and ask our team for assistance. Please visit our websites for help.
http://www.Get-Published-Get-Noticed.com/gpgn/
http://shawnchhabra.com/

Conclusion

This book is written to empower individuals to join the movement in making a positive difference in the world. You can help to share your expertise, knowledge, and skills from whatever you have learned in your own life. There is something wonderful that you have to share, and there is no better time than the present to share it and make it work for you!

This is a book dedicated to help anyone who may be having doubts or frustration in which way they should go. The hope is that by drawing inspiration from masterminds who have perhaps been through the struggles and obstacles, that you may be able to relate and find great inspiration. If others have overcome obstacles and achieved their ultimate goal, then so can you. Now you have the knowledge and inspiration to go after this very real step in the process, and you can become a published author and enjoy greater success than you ever imagined.

Since I have always been into natural healing I understand a need for wellness and well-being for the person as a whole -- body, mind and spirit. You have to be true to yourself and consider what others are truly needing, what is the root problem they are suffering from, what inhibits them from ascertaining goals they may have set for themselves and ways to help them achieve what is missing in their life, career, and family.

Do you feel energized? Do you feel informed? Are you ready to turn this information and knowledge into your own great personal success? If this sounds good, then there is no better time than the present to make it happen. My hope is that by reading about my experiences and the insight that I have gained that you will feel that push to move forward with this important step in your career. You now see just how much power publishing has within it, so harness this and turn it into something really wonderful for yourself.

I can tell you firsthand that people will know who you are, and this will give you respect and admiration from those that read your published work. You will gain personal and professional experience and visibility in a whole new way. I promise you that this will be a positive experience in more ways than you can even envision right now!

***This One Activity Can Launch Your Career Like Never
Before***

There are tremendous things that await you, and all
through making publishing a key part of your marketing
strategy. It doesn't matter how long you've been in
business, what you do, or what types of goals that you
have—for publishing can benefit all of us in a fundamental
way. I have seen it firsthand, and you will too!

I hope that you have enjoyed reading about my
experiences, but more importantly that you gained insight
into the world of publishing. Understanding how it works
and seeing the step by-step process will help you to
create your own journey, and that's often the biggest
hurdle. It all starts with an idea and some experience, and
that can quickly evolve into a book that gets published to
share with the world. So you see, it's not just celebrated
authors that can take things to the next level, you can
too!

So now you have the insight and it's time to take it to the next level, transform your ideas into a published book that you can feel proud of. Be the person that people respect, people turn to, and become a subject matter expert that the world can see. There is nothing standing in your way, so enjoy what publishing can do for you and understand that once you master this process you will take your business and your reputation to new heights—great things lie ahead so go after them!

You now have all the tools and insight from somebody just like you who once considered the notion of publishing with a bit of fear and anxiety. I have gained great success by publishing my own books, and I hope that I have helped you to see that you can do the same. **You will be amazed at what publishing can do for your overall visibility and business goals-you will enjoy greater success than you ever imagined in every sense of the word!**

Good luck and enjoy the journey to being a published author and enjoying great success through this amazing marketing and business move that will take you to new heights—enjoy every step of this wonderful process and look to better days ahead because of it!

Resources

If you are interested in writing, publishing, and therefore promoting yourself then you can learn more through our free training course. I'm going to highlight some of the best tips, but this free training can help you to decide if you want to also pursue publishing school to take it one step further.

http://www.Get-Published-Get-Noticed.com/gpgn/

We will provide you **Done-For-You, as well as Do-it-Yourself** packages.
We will help you with –

- Keyword Search
- Topic
- Title
- Writing
- Formatting
- Publishing-Digital Copies
- Publishing-Print Version
- Audio Version
- Promotion and PR
- AS-SEEN-ON- AFFILIATE NETWORKS (FOX, ABC, NBC, CBS, ETC.)
- Ongoing support

http://www.Get-Published-Get-Noticed.com/gpgn/

SPECIAL OFFER: FREE RESOURCES: We will provide you **Done-For-You, as well as Do-it-Yourself** packages.
We will help you with – Keyword Search, Topic, Title, Writing, Formatting, Publishing -Digital Copies, Publishing- Print Version, Audio Version, Promotion and PR, AS-SEEN-ON- AFFILIATE NETWORKS (FOX, ABC, NBC, CBS, ETC.), Ongoing support

http://www.Get-Published-Get-Noticed.com/gpgn/

Other Recommended Reads:

Shawn Chhabra
Five Times Best Selling Author

ABOUT THE AUTHOR

Shawn Chhabra is a successful Entrepreneur, Educator, Book Coach, Business Guru and marketing executive who resides in Saint Louis, Missouri, USA.

http://www.shawnchhabra.com

https://www.linkedin.com/in/shawnchhabrausa

If you are interested in writing, publishing, and therefore promoting yourself then you can learn more through our free training course. I'm going to highlight some of the best tips, but this free training can help you to decide if you want to also pursue publishing school to take it one step further.

http://www.Get-Published-Get-Noticed.com/gpgn/

We will provide you **Done-For-You, as well as Do-it-Yourself** packages.
We will help you with –

- Keyword Search
- Topic
- Title
- Writing
- Formatting
- Publishing-Digital Copies
- Publishing-Print Version
- Audio Version
- Promotion and PR
- AS-SEEN-ON- AFFILIATE NETWORKS (FOX, ABC, NBC, CBS, ETC.)
- Ongoing support

http://www.Get-Published-Get-Noticed.com/gpgn/

Books by Shawn Chhabra

WINNING WAY

the WINNING WAY

The World's Leading Entrepreneurs and Professionals
Share How They are
in Life and Business and How You Can Too!

the WINNING WAY

FEATURING
SHAWN CHHABRA, BRIAN TRACY
& Leading Experts from Around the World

CelebrityPress

the WINNING WAY

By definition, winning means that you competed and you came out ahead. Human nature requires us to compete in order to survive. Therefore, winning and survival have the element of success in common. To ascend to a winning position, you need a goal, a desire to achieve it, and the qualities of discipline, perseverance and action to attain it.

Having your goal and setting yourself up to achieve your goal is the first step in the process. You adjust your mindset and begin to plan diligently. Goals may be as different as DNA, but methodologies have much in common. Furthermore, your plans and expectations will need adjustments as you go along. That is why the knowledge shared by the CelebrityExperts® in this book will be of importance to you.

The advice and suggestions of these CelebrityExperts® are based on their experiences—both their accomplishments and their shipwrecks. The knowledge they share will allow you to make plans that can propel you in the right direction.

That is the function of a mentor – to guide you where you are going and to advise what to avoid.

If you wish to develop The Winning Way to your goals, read on...

You will never win if you never begin.
– Helen Rowland

CelebrityPress

LIFE STRESS TIME
MANAGEMENT

Do you feel like you are not in control of your life? Do you struggle to figure out how to get everything done in a day? Are you worried that you can´t stay organized or stay ahead of the game? If you want to take your life back and truly enjoy the time that you have, then this "Time Management" book is for you!

The "Time Management" is a book that shows you what it really means to stay in control of your life. Though you may feel bogged down by commitments and a lack of time to complete them all, sometimes it's simply a matter of staying organized. This book, written by Shawn Chhabra, can be an excellent tool in helping you to do just that.

It's Time To Take Control of Your Time and Your Life and Learn How To Do That

SHAWN CHHABRA

Sudershan Chhabra a.k.a. **Shawn Chhabra** is a successful entrepreneur, educator, business coach and marketing executive. He holds a Bachelor's and Master's degree, and places great emphasis on a solid education. Shawn is a best-selling award winning author and is featured as one of the America's PremierExpert ® at:

http://www.americaspremierexperts.com/shawn-chhabra.php

Shawn is the proud co-author of the forthcoming book "THE WINNING WAY" with Brian Tracy

Shawn is happily married to his beautiful wife, Indu and they have four wonderful children. He understands the value of family and this is his first priority in life.

http://www.shawnchhabra.com

TIME
MANAGEMENT

LIFE MANAGEMENT
STRESS MANAGEMENT
Ideas, Tools, Tips, Hints and Habits
—— Time Management Tools ——
Productivity Resources and Techniques
Healthy and Happy Lifestyle- Habits and Tips

—— *From the co-author of forthcoming book* ——
"THE WINNING WAY" WITH BRIAN TRACY

SHAWN CHHABRA